The Permaculture Student
The Workbook

Written by Matt Powers

Table of Contents

Chapter I 5
Location & Orientation

Chapter II 12
Your Site

Chapter III 24
Mainframe Planning

Chapter IV 34
Your Permaculture Design

Chapter V 45
The Designer's Mindset

1 | Location & Orientation

Where do you live?

Country _____

City/Town _____ State _____

Latitude _____ Longitude _____

Altitude _____ Distance from the Ocean _____

Size of site _____

Site Aspects _____
_____
_____
_____
_____

Steepest Slope Grade _____ % of the land over 20% Slope _____

Gentlest Slope Grade _____ % of the land under 9% Slope _____

Describe the landscape as it is:

_____
_____
_____
_____
_____
_____

A Simple Way to Calculate Slope

$$\frac{\text{Rise}}{\text{Run}} = \frac{1}{3} = 33\%$$

_____
_____
_____

Sunpath

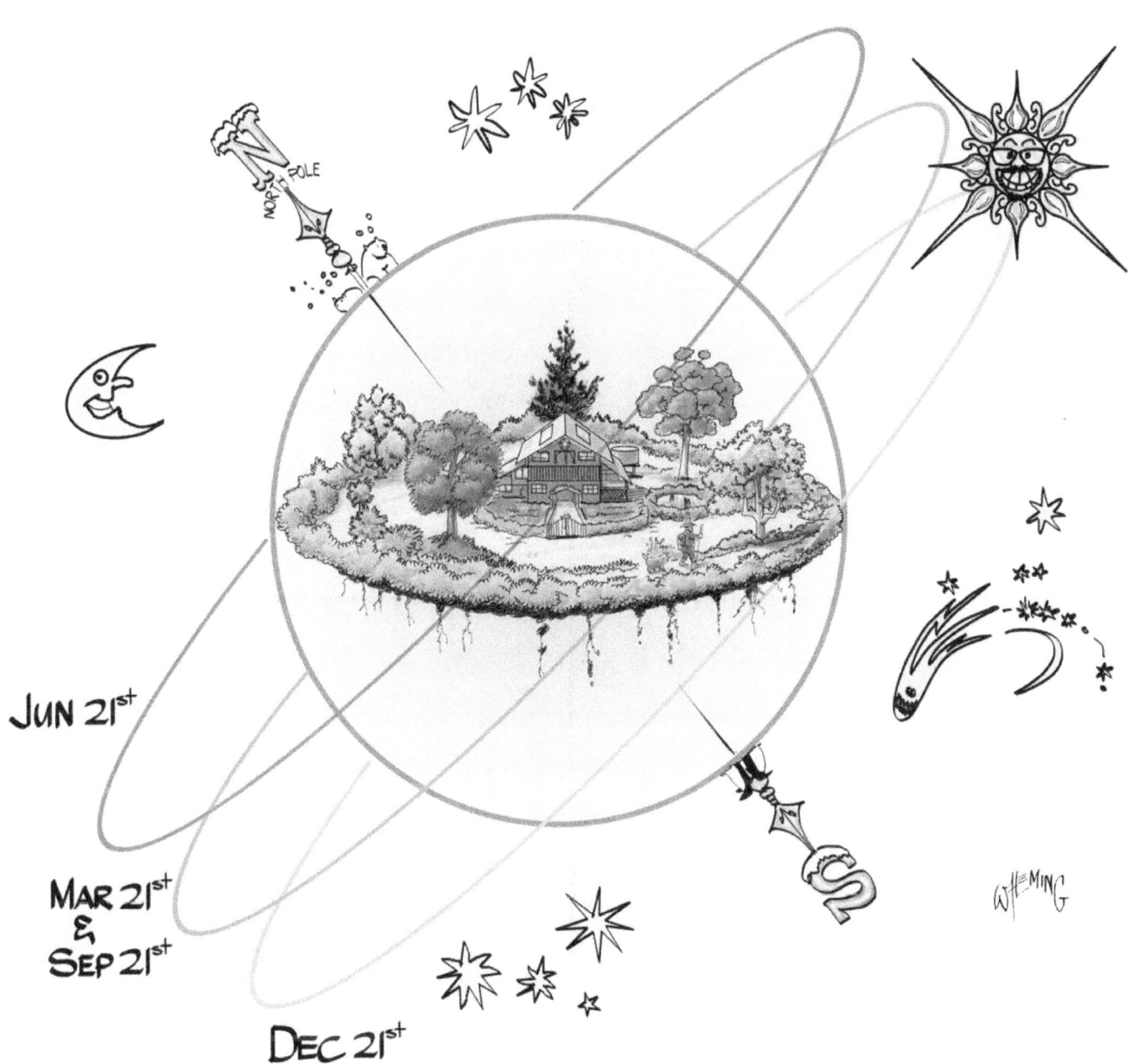

LOCATION & ORIENTATION | 7

Winter Solstice
Midday, the least light

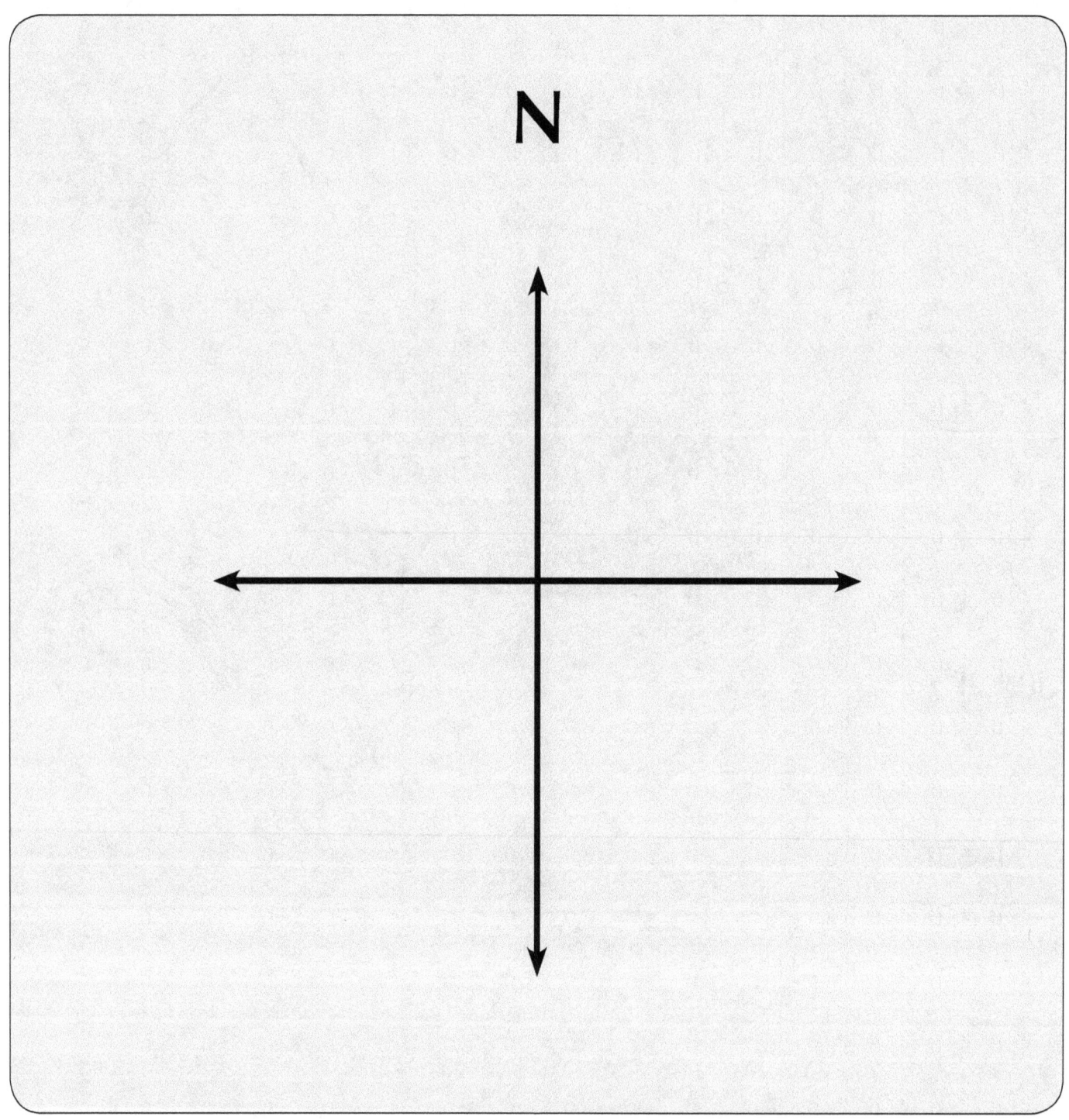

Sun Angle _____

Summer Solstice
Midday, the most light

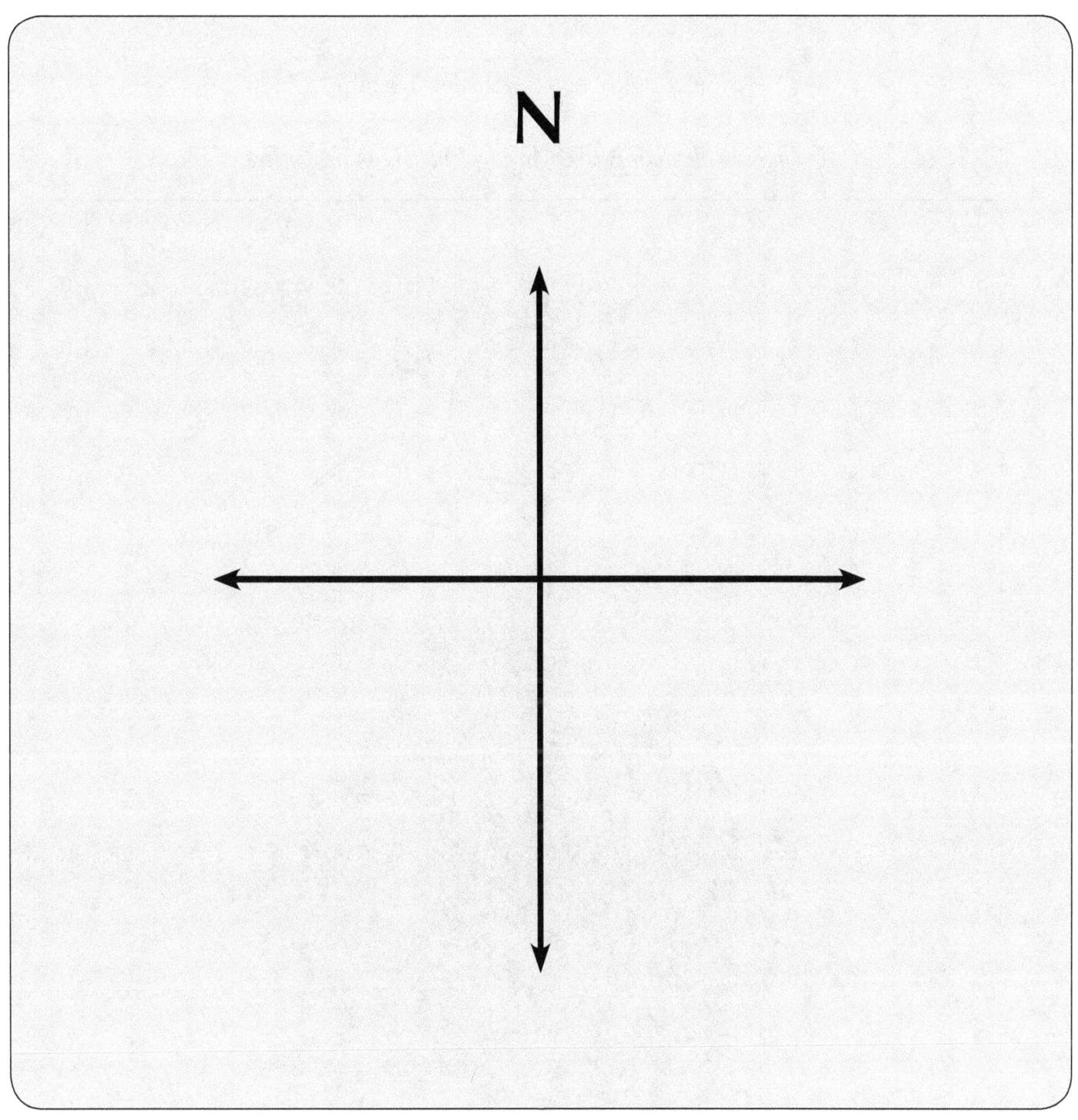

Sun Angle _____

LOCATION & ORIENTATION | 9

How to Calculate Sun Angle

Using a 1 m pole vertically on a sunny day, form a perfect 90° angle between the ground & pole. Measure the length of the shadow. Use a calculator with a TAN function and the equation:

Sun Angle = tan-1(1/Shadow Length).

The e are also Sun Path & Angle calculators online for free.

Make a Topographic Map

Use SketchUp & GoogleEarth or any other program or combination thereof to make a topographic map. It can take as little as 10 minutes to create the first time. You can also purchase topographic maps if you must. There is also a possibility that your county office of records might have a map as well.

There are in general 3 options: draw one by hand which can be very inaccurate, create one with a GPS device, a laser site and Google Earth, pay for someone to make one, or generate your own with SketchUp and GoogleEarth.

Open a new session in SketchUp, find your location on Google Earth (using longitude and latitude, address or by hand) and select your site using the Google Earth Import function. Once you have it loaded, contour it with the Topographic function.

Once contoured, generate an equivalent in size plot adjacent to your site in SketchUp and move it under or at the exact bottom of the contoured map from Google Earth. You then copy and paste it every 2-10 ft (1-2m) depending on the scale of the site upward, so that it is a solid box of layers. You then select only the interface between the layers and the contoured map. You then erase the layers. The lines will remain on the map. The best way to learn the shortcuts quickly is to watch a video online.

Search on Youtube with keywords like:
"SketchUp Google Earth Topographic"
or
Topographic Maps Online
http://mytopo.com/

II | Your Site

What is your climate? _____

What natural microclimates does your site have & how large are they?

_____
_____
_____
_____
_____
_____
_____
_____

Arid or Humid? _____ (angular or rounded landscape)

> **Temperate:** extends from the polar to the mediterranean, cool to cold.
> **Tropics:** hot and humid equatorial zone between the Tropic of Cancer and the Tropic of Capricorn
> **Dryland:** high evaporation zone found in all areas

What other areas have the same climatic conditions (or are Climate Analogs)?

_____
_____
_____
_____
_____
_____
_____
_____
_____
_____
_____
_____
_____

YOUR SITE | 13

Find a Climate Analog

There are many ways to find similar climates to any site. Using maps online, you can view just your climate analog (as on Wikipedia). You can also print them out in black and white & shade in the areas of the globe where you are similar.

Climate Map: Koppen-Geiger Climate Classification Map which can be found on Wikipedia & elsewhere.

Same latitude & altitude: Latitude can adjust as altitude adjusts (every 100m higher in altitude is equal to 1 latitudinal degree away from the equator in general, but not entirely.)

Same distance from the ocean: closer to the ocean, the more mild the winters & summers; farther from the ocean, the more intense the winters & summers.

Plant Hardiness Maps: these can serve as a general planting selection guide though microclimates always provide a stretch

What is the record rain event in your area? _____ in 24 hrs

How many centimeters/inches per minute would it be during that record rain event? _____

What is the average rainfall per month?

_____ January   _____ July
_____ February   _____ August
_____ March   _____ September
_____ April   _____ October
_____ May   _____ November
_____ June   _____ December

Total Average Annual Rainfall _____

Calculating Catchment

Using a contour map and starting from the pond site, trace at a right angle (90°) to contour until the ridge is met on both sides. The outlined area is the water catchment. Determine how many square meters the area is. Your local county records or town or city library will have the maximum rainfall historically re-corded. It is the total area times the maximum amount of possible rain that calculates the maximum flow of water. Knowing this information determines the size of the pond, the dam wall, and its level sill. This can be applied to roof catchment too.

For every 1 mm of rain that falls, it is 1 liter per square meter.

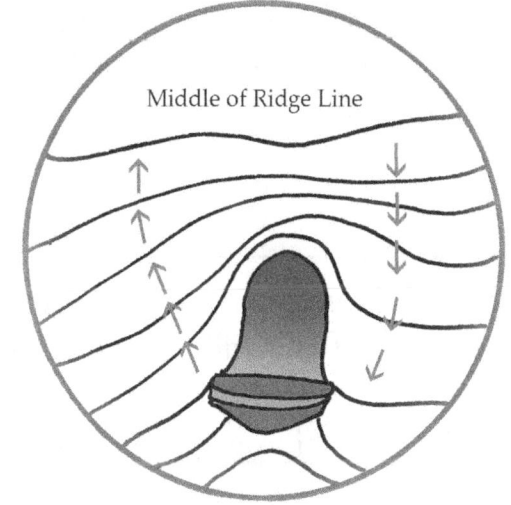
Middle of Ridge Line

LOCATION & ORIENTATION | 15

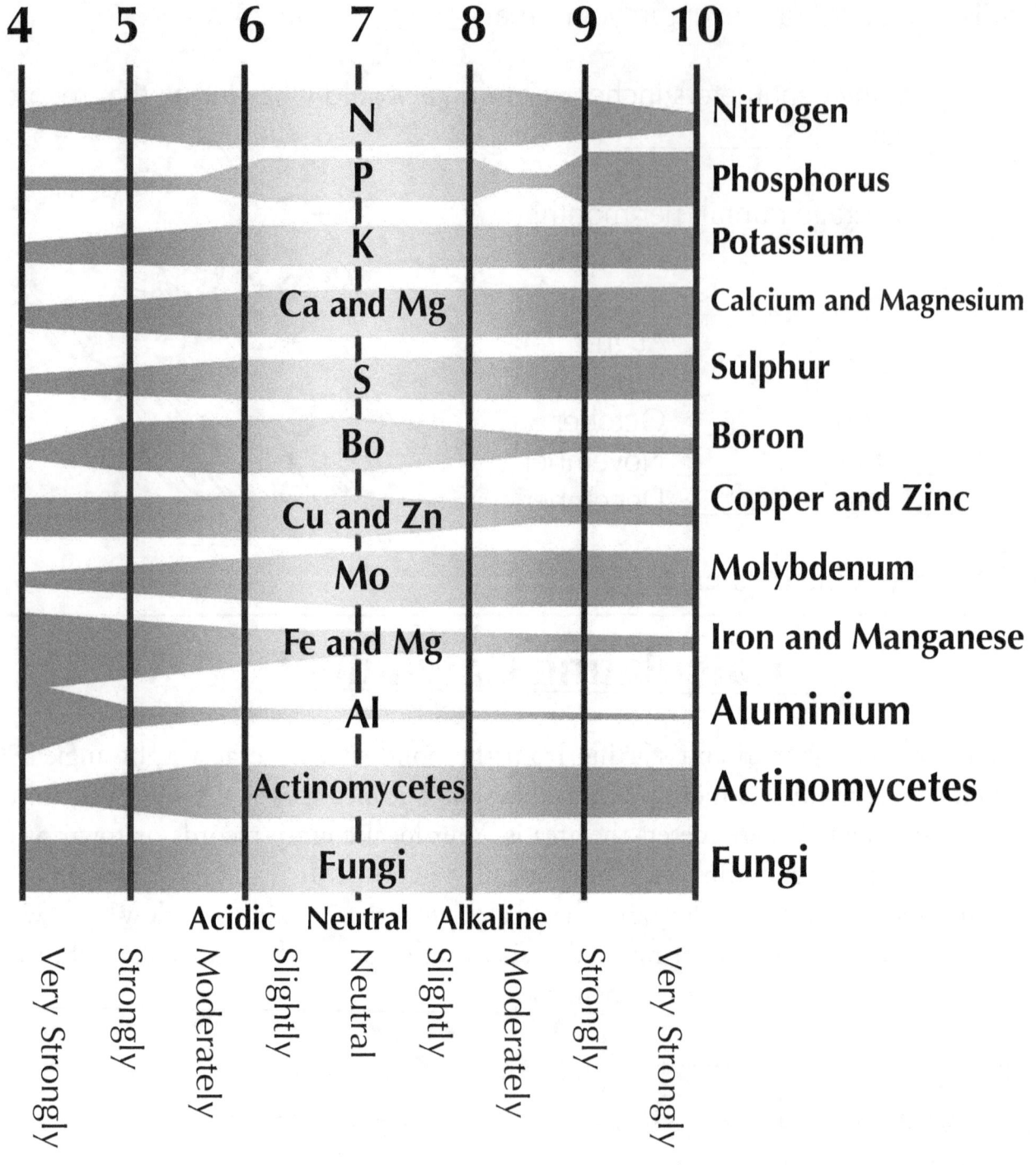

The full pH range is 1-14, but for our purposes (& soil) this chart demonstrates the ranges of pH you will likely find on a home site & shows the availability of soil nutrients & life. If we are in the 6-8 pH range we can be reasonably assured that if we have healthy soils our plants can determine their own pH levels by releasing the kind of exudates that attract the microbiology that will create that desirable pH.

What's your soil pH?

____ **Sample 1**
____ **Sample 2**
____ **Sample 3**
____ **Sample 4**
____ **Sample 5**
____ **Sample 6**
____ **Sample 7**
____ **Sample 8**
____ **Sample 9**
____ **Sample 10**

How to do a Jar Soil Test

- Fill a jar half with soil.
- Fill the rest of jar nearly to the top with water
- Securely close & shake until completely all soil is suspended in the water

Reading the Results 1
- Let settle 1 minute, mark sand level.
- Let settle 5 - 6 more hours
- Let settle 24 - 48 hours the clay level after two days.

Reading the Results 2
- Let settle 1-20 days

Draw in your own soil samples

Draw in your own soil samples

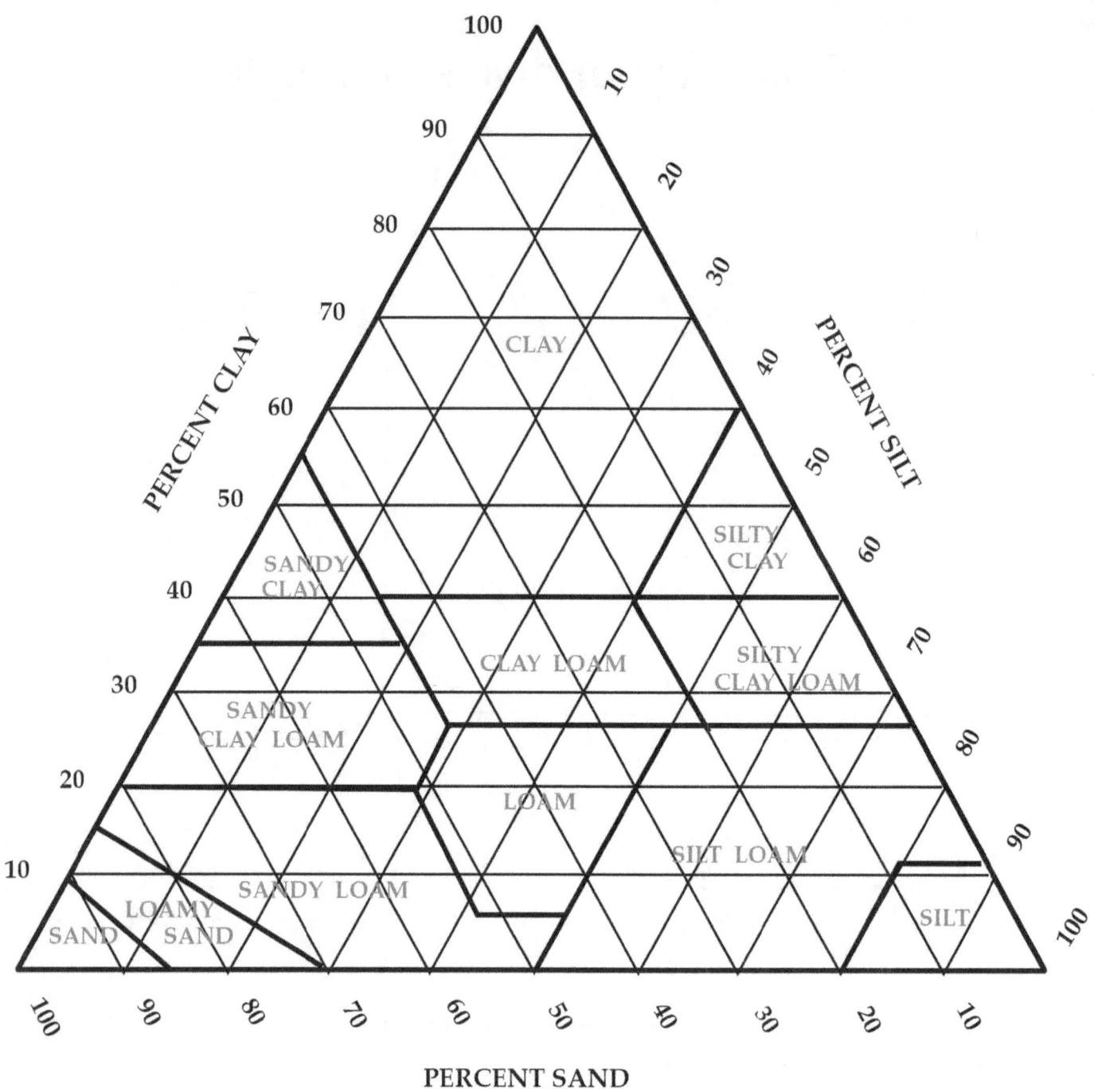

Use the Soil Chart above to determine your soil type(s). What soils are on the site?

_____
_____
_____
_____

What can be added to the soil to improve it?

_____
_____
_____
_____
_____
_____
_____
_____

What living mulch grows in your area?

_____
_____
_____
_____
_____
_____

Some possibilities for...

Acid Soils
- Compost Tea with Molasses
- Light tillage
- Add Organic Matter
- Compost &/Or Manure

Alkaline Soils
- Add Organic Matter
- Compost &/Or Manure
- Fresh Coffee Grinds
- Compost Tea with chitin and fish hydrolysate
- No Tillage
- Green Manure & Cover Crops

Mulch Plants

Depending on what is needed, many different plants can provide mulch. In general, a mulch plant is one that sheds a lot of organic material. In guilds, a nitrogen-fixing or nutrient accumulating plant is usually desired, but sometimes a pH altering plant is needed. There are databases by climate online.

Examples: Bananas, Palms, Comfrey, Artichokes, Rhubarb, Clover, Nasturtium, & more.

To find more permaculture plants for your region, consult Natural Capital Plant Database: http://permacultureplantdata.com/

What Green Manure Crops grow in your area?

_____
_____
_____
_____
_____
_____
_____

> **Green Manure Crops**
> These are perennial or annual leguminous crops planted to enrich the soil with nutrient and organic matter. They are tilled under or chopped and dropped in position by hand or with a mower. There are databases by climate online.
>
> *Examples: clover, vetch, peas, beans, etc.*
>
> To find more permaculture plants for your region, consult Natural Capital Plant Database: http://permacultureplantdata.com/

What Nitrogen fixing shrubs, bushes & trees grow in your area?

_____
_____
_____
_____
_____
_____
_____

*Remember, all soils no matter the profile can become "loam" if the organic matter is high enough & the soil life is vibrant and diverse enough. Any soil can become fertile within weeks. Just ask Dr. Elaine Ingham!

Nitrogen fixing shrubs, bushes & trees

Nitrogen fixing plants have a symbiotic relationship with bacteria and primarily use root nodules to draw nitrogen out of atmosphere. This is part of why aerated soils are beneficial, nitrogen in those pockets of air provide nitrogen. There are databases by climate online.

Examples: Siberian Pea Shrub, Black Locust, Mimosa, Acacia, etc.

Online Databases
    www.pfaf.org
    http://www.theplantlist.org/browse/A/Leguminosae/
    http://www.perennialsolutions.org/all-nitrogen-fixers-are-not-created-equal
    http://permacultureplantdata.com/

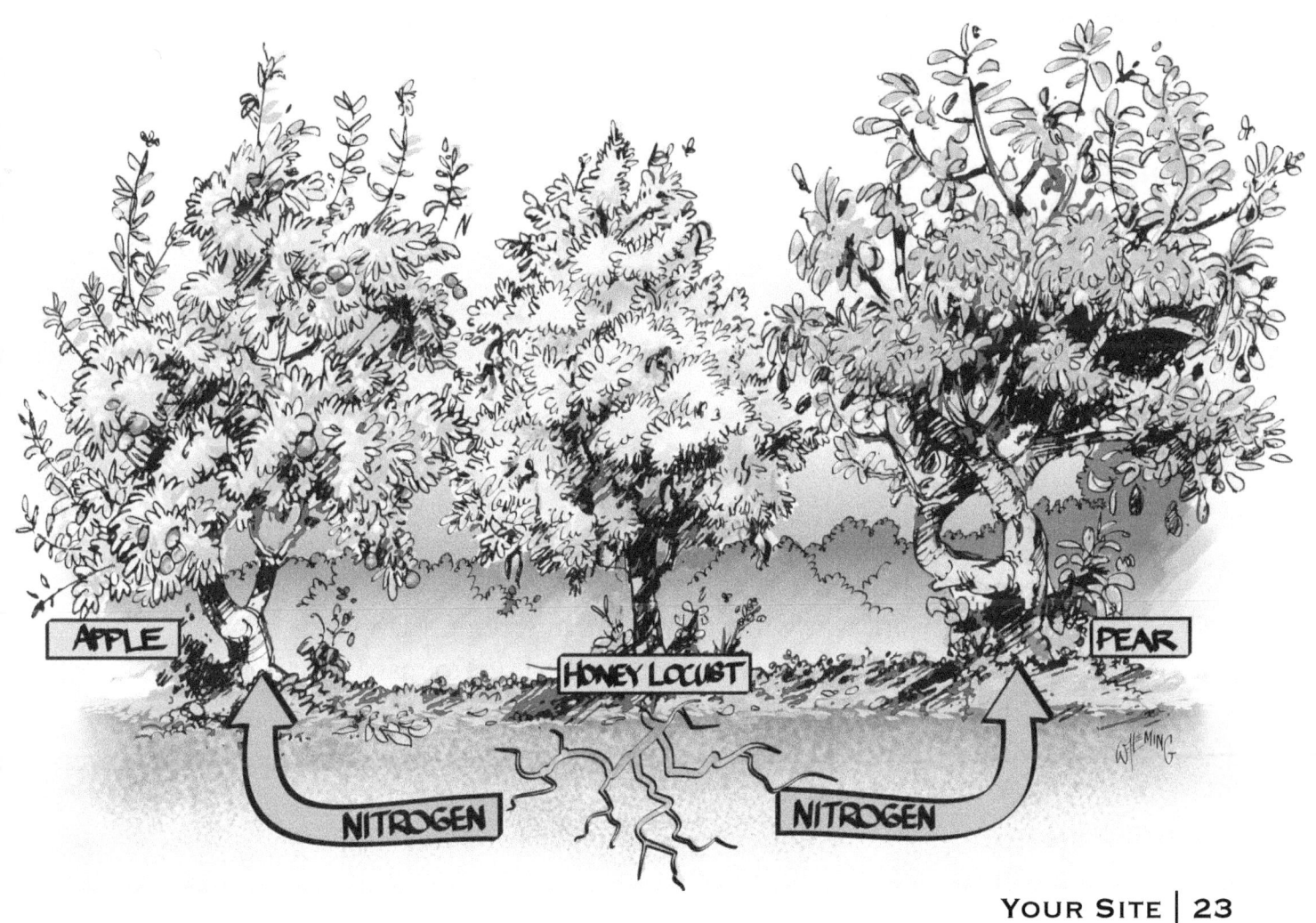

III | Mainframe Planning

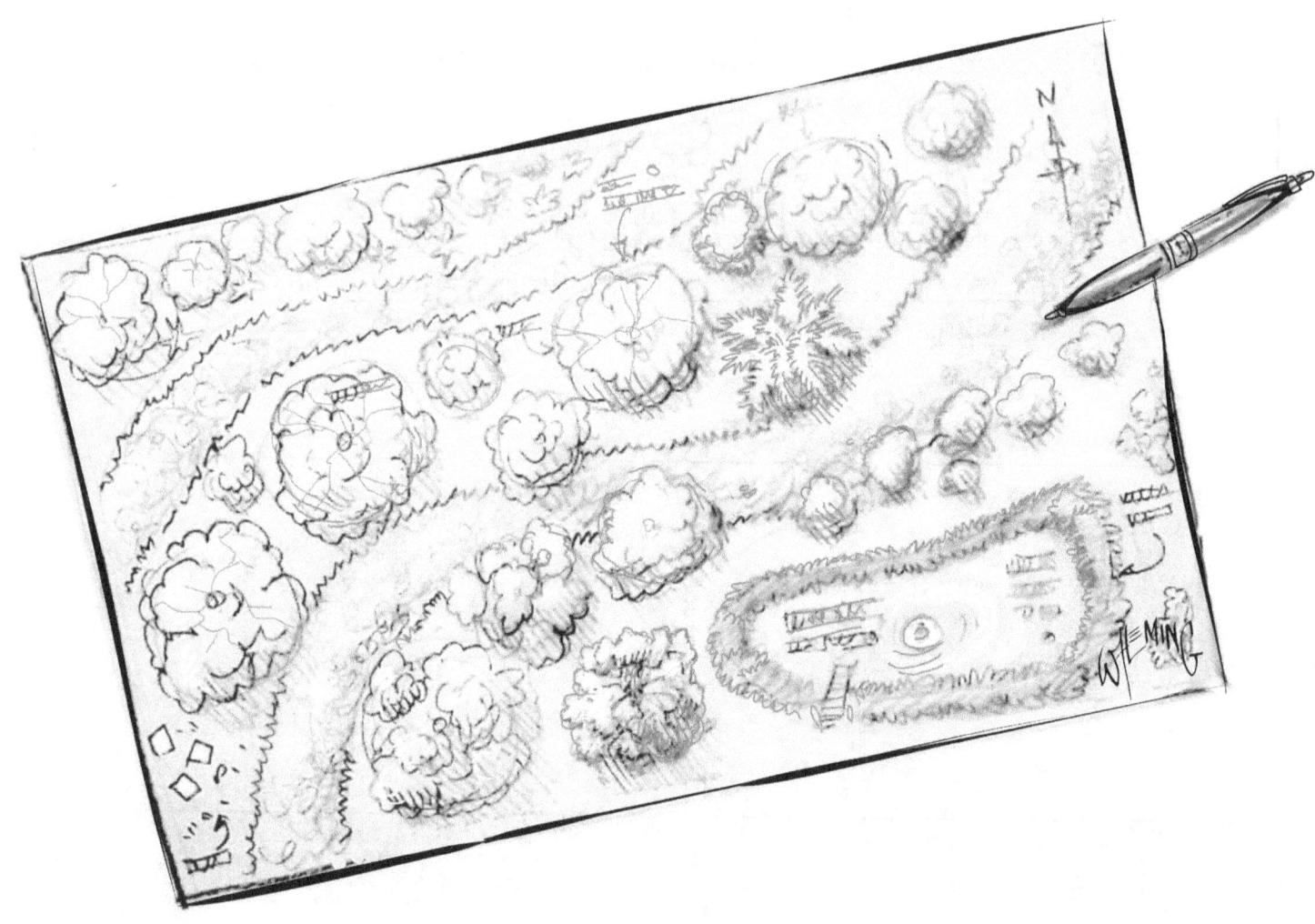

Maps work best when they come in groups. Map layers show options quickly and clearly. Feel free to make your maps inside & out of the workbook.

Using your Topographic Map...
Identify the Keypoint dam sites & the Keyline

Identify the longest, highest shortest, highest longest, lowest shortest & lowest longest contour lines of the site

Identify the Lowest Point on the Highest Boundary where water enters the property and the most productive pond/dam sites.

Identify possible Zones for your site

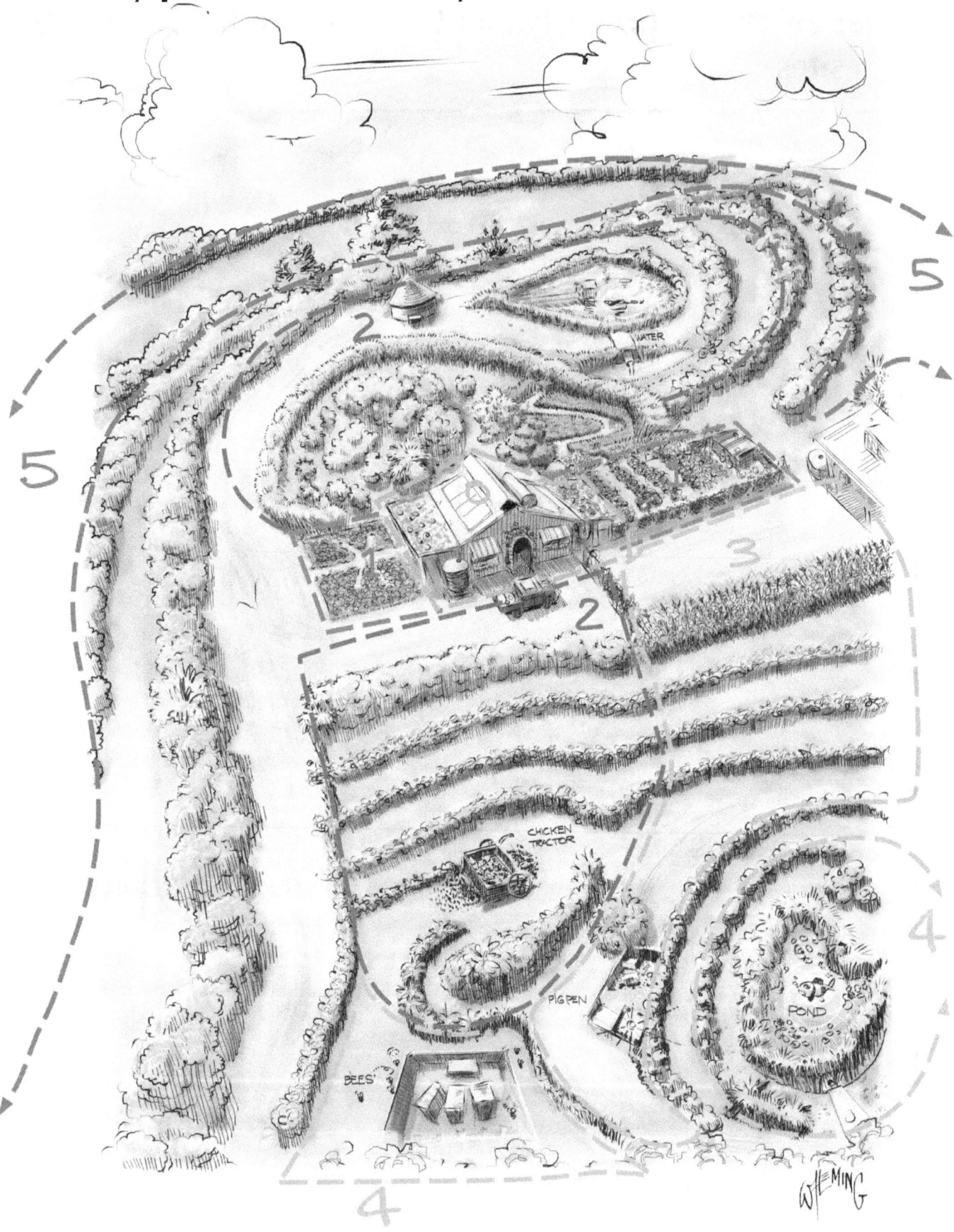

Identify & list areas with the most potential energy, shelter & sustainable energy possibilities.

Examples: Places that are in the sun all day long, wind tunnels, highest dam site, etc.

_____
_____
_____
_____
_____
_____

List the ideal broad acre crops for your site & climate

MAINFRAME PLANNING | 31

List the ideal kitchen garden crops for your site & climate

Random Assemblies

Connections can be made through random selections that can have interesting results. X and Y can be Water and Structure or some other combination.

X	Connection	Y
_____	_____	_____
_____	_____	_____
_____	_____	_____
_____	_____	_____
_____	_____	_____
_____	_____	_____
_____	_____	_____
_____	_____	_____
_____	_____	_____

IV | Your Permaculture Design

In this section layers of the same map are created, and labels are added. You can use the space provided to draw your site, copy and paste images into the space, or insert full page maps as well.

The Mainframe Design

Identify all finali ed pond, swale, earthwork, structure, main crop, kitchen garden & zone placement.

Choose animal elements & position them

_____
_____
_____
_____
_____
_____
_____
_____
_____

_____
_____
_____
_____

Design your kitchen garden & list the plants you are focusing on

Design your main crop area & list the plants you are focusing on

Forest Plans & Time Stacking

There are different types of forestry: food, timber, fruit, nut, forage, or anything else you can think of (even syrup can be a focus). There is always an initial planting that is heavily cover crop but can have all the elements of the final forest planted at the same time. The idea is to plant out the correct balance of nitrogen-fixing and mulch to valuable plants. Initially it is 90% support species and 10% valuable food forest species. At climax it can be the exact opposite where 90% of the area is taken by valuable species, and 10% is support species.

If we do not design for all the layers of forest, nature will provide, usually with a "weed". Layers can range how you classify them and where you are in the world. Typically there are 7 main layers with additional layers in specific climates: Climax or Canopy, Understory, Shrubs & Bushes, Herbs, Ground Cover, Root & Climber. There can be additional layers like understory and climax Palms in the Tropics, an additional herbaceous layer in the Cold Climate, & a Clumping layer of plants that spread by division. For organization purposes, our list is more broad to include all climate designers.

Annual Cover Crop Legumes

_____   _____

_____   _____

_____   _____

_____   _____

_____   _____

_____   _____

Root Layer

_____   _____
_____   _____
_____   _____
_____   _____
_____   _____

Climbers & Creepers

_____   _____
_____   _____
_____   _____
_____   _____
_____   _____

Herbaceous Mulch & Nitrogen-Fixing Plants

_____   _____
_____   _____
_____   _____
_____   _____
_____   _____

Short to Long Lived Support Trees, Shrubs, & Bushes

Short			MidRange			Long

_____		_____		_____

_____		_____		_____

_____		_____		_____

_____		_____		_____

_____		_____		_____

Valuable Understory Trees & Plants

_____		_____

_____		_____

_____		_____

_____		_____

_____		_____

_____		_____

YOUR PERMACULTURE DESIGN | 41

Valuable Climax or Canopy Trees

_____   _____
_____   _____
_____   _____
_____   _____
_____   _____
_____   _____

Design plant guilds for each area

_____   _____
_____   _____
_____   _____
_____   _____
_____   _____
_____   _____
_____   _____

Identify Problems that can be Solutions

_____ → _____
_____ → _____
_____ → _____
_____ → _____
_____ → _____
_____ → _____
_____ → _____
_____ → _____
_____ → _____

Aquaculture
Identify aquaculture pond sites on the map

Pond size(s) & depth(s)	Plants	Animals/Fish
1 _____	_____	_____
2 _____	_____	_____
3 _____	_____	_____
4 _____	_____	_____
5 _____	_____	_____
6 _____	_____	_____
7 _____	_____	_____
8 _____	_____	_____
9 _____	_____	_____
10 _____	_____	_____
	_____	_____

V | The Designer's Mindset

When we start down the path of permaculture design, we unintentionally open up a new way of thinking.

We see patterns everywhere.

We read landscapes.

The world of dirt becomes the world of soil.

We see that permaculture applies everywhere & solves problems that previously seemed unsolvable.

Once you have adopted a designer's mindset, you see the world with new eyes.

I invite you all to see the world as a place where humans can make it progressively better with every action we take.

MP

About the Author

Matt Powers was born in '82 in CT. Matt grew up skiing, drawing & playing outside. He has a BA from New York University in British & American Literature, a MA in Education from National University & a permaculture design certificate from Geoff Lawton's online course. Matt was a musician, teaching, touring & recording in studios in NYC & LA in his 20s. He married Adriana & had two sons. After Adriana got cancer twice in one year, the family relocated to California. After a few years more of touring and recording, Matt started subbing & then teaching English & Digital Music Production in a Central Valley California public charter school, Minarets.us, that focused on student-centered learning, technology & community building.

Currently Matt works with the Baker Creek Heirloom Seed company, speaks at teaching, farming, & permaculture conferences about permaculture, seeds, & the future of farming and education. He is also host of the Permaculture Tonight podcast on iTunes & SoundCloud.

Websites:
thepermaculturestudent.com
twitter.com/Permaculture123
facebook.com/ThePermacultureStudent
facebook.com/PermacultureTonight
soundcloud.com/PermacultureTonight

Other Titles by Matt Powers
The Magic Beans
The Permaculture Student 2
Permaculture for School Gardens

Looking for More?

Visit ThePermacultureStudent.com for FREE Instruction & Ebooks, Online Courses, Advanced & Beginner Books, Podcast Episodes, Blog Posts, & More!

Grow Abundantly, Learn Daily, & Live Regeneratively,

Matt Powers

www.ingramcontent.com/pod-product-compliance
Lightning Source LLC
Chambersburg PA
CBHW080415300426
44113CB00015B/2528